SCIENCE ANSWERS
Life Processes
FROM REPRODUCTION TO RESPIRATION

Louise and Richard Spilsbury

www.heinemann.co.uk/library
Visit our website to find out more information about **Heinemann Library** books.

To order:
☎ Phone 44 (0) 1865 888066
▤ Send a fax to 44 (0) 1865 314091
▭ Visit the Heinemann Bookshop at www.heinemann.co.uk/library to browse our catalogue and order online.

First published in Great Britain by
Heinemann Library, Halley Court,
Jordan Hill, Oxford OX2 8EJ,
part of Harcourt Education.

Heinemann is a registered trademark of
Harcourt Education Ltd.

Editorial: Nancy Dickmann and Tanvi Rai
Design: Richard Parker and Celia Floyd
Picture Research: Rebecca Sodergren and
Pete Morris
Production: Séverine Ribierre

Originated by Dot Gradations Ltd
Printed in China by WKT
Company Limited

ISBN 0 431 17516 0 (hardback)
08 07 06 05 04
10 9 8 7 6 5 4 3 2 1

ISBN 0 431 17523 3 (paperback)
09 08 07 06 05
10 9 8 7 6 5 4 3 2 1

**British Library Cataloguing
in Publication Data**
Spilsbury, Louise and Richard
Life Processes. – (Science Answers)
571
A full catalogue record for this book is
available from the British Library.

Acknowledgements
The publishers would like to thank the
following for permission to reproduce
photographs: Corbis **p. 4**; Corbis/Wally
McNamee **p. 15**; FLPA/Minden Pictures
pp. 5, **22**; FLPA/R. Van Nostrand **p. 25**;
FLPA/Sunset **p. 16**; FLPA/Terry
Andrewartha **p. 13**; Harcourt Education
Ltd/Robert Lifson **p. 9**; Harcourt Education
Ltd/Tudor Photography **pp. 14, 23, 27**;
Nature Picture Library **p. 29**;
NHPA/Anthony Bannister **pp. 19, 21**;
NHPA/Martin Harvey **p. 8**; NHPA/Stephen
Dalton **p. 12**; Science Photo Library/Adam
Hart-Davis **p. 24**; Science Photo
Library/Andrew Syred **p. 17**; Science Photo
Library/Dr Jeremy Burgess **p. 7**; Science
Photo Library/Gregory Ochocki **p. 11**;
Science Photo Library/Gusto **p. 10**; Science
Photo Library/James King-Holmes **p. 28**;
Science Photo Library/John Mitchell **p. 26**;
Science Photo Library/Lynwood Chase **p.
20**; Science Photo Library/Peter Chadwick
p. 18; Science Picture Library/Science
Pictures Limited **p. 6**.

Cover photograph of a whiptail wallaby
joey in mother's pouch reproduced with
permission of Corbis/Martin Harvey.

Every effort has been made to contact copyright
holders of any material reproduced in this book. Any
omissions will be rectified in subsequent printings if
notice is given to the publishers.

The paper used to print this book comes from
sustainable resources.

Contents

What are life processes? 4

What is reproduction? 6

How do living things grow? 9

How do living things feed? 11

What is respiration? 15

How do living things get rid of waste? 18

Can all living things move? 20

What are senses? 24

People who found the answers 28

Amazing facts 29

Glossary 30

Index 32

More books to read 32

Any words appearing in bold, **like this**, are explained in the Glossary.

About the experiments and demonstrations

This book contains some boxes headed 'Science Answers'. Each one describes an experiment or demonstration that you can try yourself. There are some simple safety rules to follow when doing an experiment:

- Ask an adult to help with any cutting using a sharp knife.
- Wash your hands after handling plants or soil.

Materials you will use

Most of the experiments and demonstrations in this book can be done with objects that you can find in your own home and food you can buy cheaply from a shop. You will also need a pencil and paper to record your results.

What are life processes?

Life processes are activities that all living things must do to live and thrive. The incredible number and variety of living things on Earth look and behave very differently, but they all carry out seven basic life processes.

The seven life processes

All of the seven life processes are equally important:

- movement – the ability to move
- **respiration** – the process by which **organisms** (living things) release **energy** from their food
- sensitivity – the ability to sense and respond to changes in the world
- growth – all living things tend to start off small and get bigger
- **reproduction** – the ability to produce offspring or young
- excretion – living things release, or excrete, waste products to keep healthy
- **nutrition** – the ability to get energy from food.

Seven out of seven

Cars and buses may move and excrete waste from exhausts, but they are not living things. Living things carry out all seven life processes.

What are cells?

All living things are made up of **cells**. Cells are like tiny building blocks of life. Each cell is capable of carrying out life processes, such as taking in food, growing and reproducing. Some tiny organisms, such as an amoeba, are made up of only one cell. Large, more complex organisms, such as people or trees, are made up of many cells. Some cells have particular features so that they can perform different life processes. For example, many animals have **muscle** cells that help them move.

Dead or alive?

The corals that form a layer at the top of a reef may look dead, but they are in fact the oldest living animals on Earth. Some coral reefs are over 3000 years old.

What is reproduction?

Every species (type) of living thing can make new **organisms** similar to themselves. This is called **reproduction**. Without reproduction, all species would die out. Reproduction happens in different ways.

Identical copies

Reproduction involving just one parent is called **asexual reproduction**. Part of the parent breaks off, or a bud grows on its surface and then drops off. The new piece or bud develops into an identical copy of its parent.

New buddy?

A hydra is a tiny animal, made up of a few cells, that lives in water. In this picture, you can see a tiny new hydra budding off from a hydra's side as it reproduces asexually.

Asexual reproduction happens in a wide range of simple organisms made up of one or just a few **cells**. For example, single-celled **bacteria** reproduce by splitting into two. It also happens in more complicated organisms such as flowering plants. For example, strawberry plants produce long shoots with tiny new plants attached. Once the new plant takes root in the soil, it separates from its parent.

Merging together

Sexual reproduction is when special cells from a male and a female of the same species merge together to make a new organism. In many animals, male sex cells are called sperm and female sex cells are called eggs. When a male sex cell and a female sex cell join together, they create a new cell, and this is called **fertilization**. This cell then starts to grow into a new individual, which shows characteristics of both its parents.

Fertilization happens in flowering plants by **pollination**. This is when male sex cells, called **pollen**, move from the male parts of a flower to the female parts of the same or another flower. Here, the pollen fertilizes an egg so that it grows into a seed, which may grow into a new plant.

Passing pollen

Pollen may be blown by the wind, washed by water or carried by insects or birds from flower to flower. Bees accidentally pick up pollen on their hairy bodies when they visit flowers to feed on **nectar**.

Animal fertilization

Male animals fertilize eggs in two main ways – outside or inside the female. Female fish and frogs lay lots of eggs in water. Males then spray their sperm on to the eggs. Male **mammals**, birds and insects put their sperm on to eggs inside the female. This is called mating.

Hatching out

Some baby animals, like this crocodile, hatch out of eggs that their mothers have laid. Others, including mammals, grow safely inside their mother's body. Mammals also make food – milk – and care for their babies once they are born.

Successful reproduction

Reproduction is successful if fertilized eggs grow into new adults capable of reproduction. Living things use different ways of making sure reproduction is successful. For example, flowers look colourful, smell good and make sweet nectar to attract animals that will carry off their pollen. Seeds protect the tiny new organism inside from damage and provide a source of food to help it grow. Flowers often make lots of seeds so at least a few may succeed.

How do livings things grow?

All living things grow by increasing the number of **cells** they have and by increasing the size of the cells they already have.

More cells

Organisms get the **energy** their cells need to divide and grow from food. First, cells divide into two and each smaller identical cell increases in size. Then the two cells divide into four, four into eight and so on.

As the number of cells increases, some start to differentiate. This means that they change in order to take on different tasks for the organism. For example, some cells of the same type work together in **tissue** such as **muscle**. Several kinds of tissues make up **organs** such as the heart in some animals, or leaves in plants, which carry out particular life processes.

Getting bigger

All living things grow. As hermit crabs grow, they find bigger shells of dead sea snails to live in, because they do not form their own shells like other crabs do.

Genes and growth

Young organisms grow to be like their parent or parents because of the **genes** passed on in **reproduction**. Genes are like a cell's instruction manual, telling it how it should grow. New individuals produced by **asexual reproduction** have identical genes to their parent. Young organisms produced by **sexual reproduction** grow from a cell that contains genes from both parents.

Growing and changing

Frogs start life as water-living tadpoles. As their cells divide and grow, they form different body parts and the tadpoles change into land-living frogs.

Ways of growing

Organisms grow in different ways. Some babies, such as fox cubs, look like little versions of their parents. Others change in appearance as well as size as they grow. For example, the tadpoles that hatch from frogs' eggs look nothing like the adult frogs they will become. Some organisms, such as humans, grow until they are adults and then stop growing. Others, including plants, carry on growing until they die.

How do living things feed?

All living things take in food. This is called **nutrition**. Living things use food to supply **energy** for their bodies to carry out life processes. Plants are called producers, because they produce (make) food. Animals are consumers. They consume (eat) plants, or other animals that eat plants.

How do plants make food?

Plants use **carbon dioxide**, a gas in the air, and water to make their food. They take in carbon dioxide through holes in their leaves called **stomata** (see page 17). They take in water through their roots. Plant leaves absorb sunlight and use its energy to combine the carbon dioxide and water, turning them into energy-rich foods, such as sugars. This process is called **photosynthesis**. When plants take in water, they also take in **nutrients** dissolved in soil.

Light feeders

Kelp is a seaweed that grows in deep water. Its long leaf-like fronds grow up towards the light so that it can carry out photosynthesis. Here you can also see a California sea lion swimming between the enormous fronds.

Energy for animals

Animals cannot make their own food as plants do. They have to eat other things to get the nutrients they need. Herbivores are animals that feed mainly on plant parts, such as leaves, seeds, berries or nuts. Carnivores are animals that eat other animals. Some carnivores hunt their **prey**. For example, many spiders lay a trap – a sticky web that catches insects for them to eat. Omnivores are animals that eat both plants and animals.

What is a food chain?

The Sun is the source of all energy for living things on Earth. A food chain always begins with green plants because they can trap this energy in photosynthesis. The next link in the chain is a herbivore, which eats the plants. Then a carnivore eats the herbivore, and so on. Each plant or animal is like a link in the chain, and some energy is passed from one link to the next.

How do other organisms feed?

Most **bacteria** break down their food using chemicals, and then absorb the tiny pieces through their **cell** walls. Some bacteria, called cyanobacteria, make food by photosynthesis. Some **protists**, such as those that form part of ocean **plankton**, make food by photosynthesis too. Other protists, such as amoeba, surround food such as bacteria and digest it while they have it trapped. **Fungi**, such as mushrooms, take in nutrients from the dead wood and leaves they grow on.

Why do living things need water?

Water is a vital part of nutrition. The bodies of living things are made up mostly of water. To be healthy and able to carry out their vital life processes, most living things need to take in some water every day.

A changing diet

Some animals eat different foods at different stages of life. Mammals drink their mother's milk as babies, but eat the same food as their parents when they are older.

13

INVESTIGATION: Find out how plants take water up through their stems to the leaves to carry out photosynthesis.

EQUIPMENT:

Celery stalk with leaves still on, an empty jar, a bottle of ink or food colouring and a knife.

INVESTIGATION STEPS:

1 Put some water in the bottom of the jar.
2 Add a few drops of ink or food colouring to the water.
3 Slice a narrow piece from the end of the celery and stand the stick in the jar of coloured water. Leave it in a warm, light spot for a day.
4 Wash the end of the celery, cut it into wide slices and look at the stem.
5 Write down what you see.
6 Throw the celery stalk away after the investigation.

CONCLUSION:

All plants need water to be able to make their own food. They take it through their roots and up their stems into their leaves. The coloured spots you can see in the cut stem of celery are the tubes through which the plant carries water up to its leaves.

14

What is respiration?

Respiration is the process by which living things release the **energy** from their food. Respiration goes on in every **cell** in an **organism**'s body.

How does respiration work?

For a car to start, it has to burn its fuel – petrol – with **oxygen** to produce energy. Most living things release energy from their fuel – food – by using oxygen in a similar way. In respiration, sugars from food are combined with oxygen within each of the organism's cells. This releases energy that the cells can use to divide and grow, to repair themselves and to carry out all the other life processes.

Some organisms, such as yeast and **bacteria**, are able to release all the energy from their food without oxygen.

Releasing energy

When sprinters race down a track, their muscle cells are using energy released from food by the process of respiration.

Breathing

Breathing is an important part of the respiration process. Living things need to take in a constant supply of oxygen from the air for respiration. Many animals get oxygen by breathing it in. They breathe out to release **carbon dioxide** from their bodies. Carbon dioxide is a waste gas produced by plants and animals in the process of respiration.

Lungs and gills

Living things have different **organs** for obtaining oxygen. Many animals, including humans, have **lungs**. When we breathe, muscles in the body force air into the lungs. The lungs extract oxygen from the air and blood carries it to the body's cells. Fish have **gills** with thin **blood vessels** that take in oxygen dissolved in the water and release carbon dioxide after respiration.

Blowhole breathing

The blowhole on the top of a whale's head is the part it uses to breathe oxygen in, and carbon dioxide out, when it visits the water's surface.

How do plants get oxygen?

Plants produce some of the oxygen they need for respiration in the process of **photosynthesis**. They also take in oxygen in through their **stomata**. Stomata are tiny holes found mainly on the underside of leaves and they allow a plant to 'breathe'. This magnified (enlarged) picture shows the stomata on a leaf.

Plants can open and close their stomata using the two kidney-shaped cells that border the opening. Oxygen for respiration passes into the leaf through the stomata.

Plants also absorb some oxygen dissolved in the water they take up through their roots.

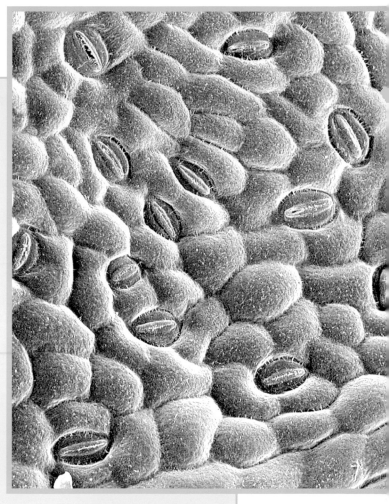

Saving up energy

Plants store some of the food they make in underground plant parts, such as a root or underground stem. Potatoes and carrots are plant food stores. When the plant needs energy, perhaps to grow again in spring after resting through winter, it uses respiration to release energy from the stored food.

How do living things get rid of waste?

All living things produce waste when they carry out life processes, such as **respiration**, in **cells**. Some of the waste is harmful, or even poisonous, if it builds up. Excretion – getting rid of waste – is an important life process.

Nutrition waste

Living things need different **nutrients** such as fat, water and **protein**. For example, cells need protein to grow and repair themselves. When cells use protein, they use parts of it but not others, leaving some waste. Urea is a type of waste protein. In some animals, such as fish and **mammals**, urea is excreted mostly using the kidneys. Kidneys are **organs** that sieve out waste and unwanted water from blood. Urine is the mixture of water and urea that animals get rid of.

Plants also produce waste from **nutrition**. Many trees move this waste inside cells of old leaves. The waste is disposed of when the leaves drop off.

Animal waste

This southern black-backed gull in South Africa is standing on a rock stained by guano. Guano is a sticky type of urine produced by sea birds.

Other waste

Animals such as mammals also produce solid waste called faeces. Faeces contain the waste bits of food, such as fibre, that an animal's body cannot **digest** (break down and make use of).

Waste gases

The **carbon dioxide** waste released during the process of respiration could poison living things if it remained in their bodies. Insects excrete it through holes on the sides of their bodies called spiracles. Many other animals use **gills** or **lungs**. When they breathe, they exchange unwanted carbon dioxide for **oxygen**.

Recycling waste

Waste from one **organism** is often essential for others. For example, when green plants make sugar by **photosynthesis**, they also excrete oxygen. Most living things require oxygen to release **energy** from their food.

Dung beetles roll faeces (dung) underground to lay their eggs on. The young dung beetles that hatch eat some, but most of the dung rots, releasing nutrients into the soil that other organisms can use.

Can all living things move?

All living things have the ability to move. It may be difficult to see **organisms** such as plants moving, but it does happen.

How do plants move?

Plants mainly move as they grow. Plant parts such as branches, roots and flowers move into new space as they get bigger. Petals on some flowers close up at night-time. This protects the delicate parts inside, used for **reproduction**, from the cold. **Pollen** from plants moves in the wind or travels on the back of insects such as bees. Seeds use various ways of moving away from their parent plant, so they can find space to grow. Some seeds grow in **fruits** that are eaten by animals and get carried away. Some seeds grow in special dry fruits that are easily blown and carried along by the wind.

Parachuting seeds

Dandelion seeds have fluffy tops that act like tiny parachutes, carrying the seeds through the air on even the gentlest of breezes.

A fast-moving plant!

Most plant movement is so slow and gradual that we cannot see it happening. However, the Venus's flytrap is an unusual plant that can move quite quickly. When an insect lands on its leaves, they snap shut, trapping the **prey** inside the plant. The Venus's flytrap then **digests** the fly so that it can absorb **nutrients**, which it cannot get from the soils in which it usually grows.

Why do animals move?

Animals move mainly to carry out the other life processes. For example, most have to move to find or catch their food. They move in order to find a partner for **reproduction**, or to get food for their young. Animals also move to escape danger – for example, rabbits run to escape being caught by foxes. Some animals move in special ways that are suited to where they live. The Peringuey's adder 'sidewinder' snake travels quickly across a desert using a special S-shaped movement to keep most of its body off the burning sand.

How do animals move?

Animals move in many different ways. Humans and many other animals have **muscles** that pull on the bones in their skeleton to make their bodies move. Animals without bones move in different ways. An earthworm's muscles lengthen and shorten its body to make it move, whilst hairs on its body grip the soil. Muscles in a jellyfish open and close its bell-shaped body, taking in water and then pushing it out again to propel the animal forward.

How do other organisms move?

Some **protists**, such as amoeba, move by stretching their jelly-like bodies across a surface. Others have special features like a thin, long hair or many hairs, which they move to and fro to swim. Parts of **fungi** move as they grow, such as the mass of threads that grow out of a toadstool's base into dead wood and leaves.

How do birds fly?

Birds, like these flamingos, have muscles in their bodies that pull on their wing muscles to help them fly.

DEMONSTRATION: To show how plant parts move.

EQUIPMENT:

A glass jar, a paper towel, and a bean seed (a broad bean seed, for example) that has been soaked in water for a day.

DEMONSTRATION STEPS:

1 Wet the paper towel with water. Fold it and wrap it around the inside of the jar.
2 Slide the bean down between the inside of the jar and the paper towel (so you can see it from the outside of the glass jar).
3 Stand the jar on a windowsill and leave it for a week or two. Keep the paper damp by adding a few drops of water if necessary.
4 Write down what you see.

EXPLANATION:

When the bean seed starts to grow, its root grows from one end and a shoot grows from the other. The bean may stay still, but the root moves down the inside of the jar and the shoot moves up the jar as it grows. This proves that plant parts can move!

What are senses?

Sensitivity is a living thing's ability to respond to **stimuli** in its surroundings – to understand and react to things in the world around them. Humans have five senses – sight, hearing, smell, taste and touch – to help them respond to their world.

Do plants have sensitivity?

Plants react to fewer stimuli than humans and other animals, but they clearly do respond to their surroundings. When a seed germinates (starts to grow), it does not matter which way up it landed in the soil; its roots always grow down and its shoots always grow up. Plant roots grow down into the soil, where they will be able to get the water the plant needs, because they respond to **gravity**. Meanwhile, plant shoots and stems grow up out of the soil, where they will be able to hold leaves up to the Sun for **photosynthesis**, because they respond to light.

Reaching for the light

These tomato seedlings (young plants) are leaning over to one side because they are growing towards the light.

Can plants touch?

Some climbing plants do respond to touch. If their stem touches another plant, or other possible support, they wrap around it. This allows them to grow up towards the light without growing strong stems for support.

How do animal senses work?

The **organs** responsible for the five human senses are the eyes, ears, nose, taste buds and skin. Most animals have some or all of these sense organs. Most sense organs are on the head, so that they are close to the brain, the organ that interprets the information they collect. For example, your eyes see a car coming and pass the information to your brain, which tells you it is not safe to cross the road. Messages from sense organs travel to the brain through **nerves**.

Night vision

Many animals that are active at night, such as this slender loris, have extra-large eyes to help them see.

Using animal senses

Animals use their senses to do many things, such as find food or escape danger. Different animals rely on different senses as their main source of information.

Bats find food in the dark by echolocation. This is when they make high squeaks (that we cannot hear) and listen to the echoes to work out where an insect is. Some rattlesnakes have hollows on their head that contain heat-sensing cells, which help them find warm-bodied **prey**, such as mice, in the dark. Fish and tadpoles have a line along their sides that senses vibrations (movements) in the water, to tell them if food or danger is nearby. Cats' whiskers help them feel their way around in the dark.

What are antennae?

Insect antennae are very special sense organs that can sense touch, scent and taste! Male Luna moths, like this one, have very large antennae to pick up the special scent females give off.

DEMONSTRATION: To show that plants sense and respond to light.

EQUIPMENT:
Cardboard box, stiff card, sticky tape, scissors and a small runner bean plant (with just two leaves) growing in a small pot.

DEMONSTRATION STEPS:
1 Stick flaps of card inside the box to create a maze (see picture below).
2 Once dry, stand the box up, put the bean plant at the bottom, make a 3-centimetre hole in the top and put the lid on tight.
3 Stand the box in a sunny spot. Take the lid off once a day for three weeks to check the plant. Water the soil if not moist. Write down what you see.

EXPLANATION:
After one to three weeks, the runner bean manages to grow round the obstacles and out of the hole at the top of the box. Plant stems sense and then grow towards light, which their leaves need to absorb to be able to make food.

Gregor Mendel (1822–84)

Mendel (pictured here) was an Austrian monk who noticed that sweet-pea seeds grew into plants that looked partly like each parent plant. By **pollinating** lots of sweet-pea flowers with each other, he worked out the way in which characteristics of parents are passed on to their young. Many years after his death, Mendel's writings about his experiments were used by other scientists to study the way that **genes** work.

Anton van Leeuwenhoek (1632–1723)

Leeuwenhoek was born in the Netherlands. He owned a cloth shop, but his hobby was making microscopes! Using these homemade microscopes he examined cloth fibres, but he later moved on to leaves, bees and other living things. He discovered what **cells** in blood, hair and skin look like close-up. Although microscopes had been invented before Leeuwenhoek, he was the first person to use them for careful scientific study.

Amazing facts

- The biggest trees in the world are the giant redwoods, which can weigh up to 2500 tonnes.

- The blue whale (see picture) is the largest animal in the world, weighing in at about 100–130 tonnes.

- Some types of bamboo plants can grow nearly 90 centimetres in a single day!

- The oldest living thing in the world is a tree that is almost 4800 years old!

- Queen driver ants may produce 3 million eggs each month.

- Some aphids take only 4 days after hatching from eggs to become adults. However, some beetles may take 40 years.

- Giant squids have eyes up to 37 centimetres across.

- To keep skin sensitive to touch, human skin **cells** constantly die, fall off and are replaced by new ones. On average, it takes about 4 years for a person to lose his or her own weight in skin!

- The Rafflesia flower is the largest in the world. A single bloom can weigh 4 kilograms and measure 90 centimetres across.

▷○ Glossary

asexual reproduction when an organism reproduces by creating another living thing from a part of itself

bacteria tiny living things found everywhere. Some bacteria can cause disease.

blood vessels tubes in the body that carry blood

carbon dioxide gas in the air around us used by plants in photosynthesis

cells building blocks of living things, so small they can only be seen with a microscope. Most plants and animals are made up of millions of cells.

digest to break down food into tiny pieces so that it can pass into the blood

energy the power that all living things need in order to live and grow and do everything that they do

fertilization when a male cell joins a female cell to make a new cell. The new cell then grows into a new living thing.

fruit part of a plant in which seeds develop

fungi group of living things including mushrooms, toadstools, yeast and moulds

genes special code carried in each of your cells that determines how they grow

gills body parts that allow an animal to breathe underwater

gravity force that makes things fall when we drop them and that stops us from floating off into space

lungs respiratory organs that breathe in air and take in oxygen from it

mammals group of animals that includes humans. All mammals feed their babies milk from their own bodies and have some hair.

muscles parts of the body that help to make the bones and the rest of the body move

nectar sugary substance plants make in their flowers to attract insects, which eat it

nerves nerves act like the body's telephone system. They carry messages from the rest of the body to and from the brain in the form of electrical signals.

nutrients chemicals that plants and animals need in order to be healthy

nutrition feeding. Living things need to obtain and use food to live.

organ part of the body that has a particular function, such as the brain, ear or eye

organism living thing

oxygen gas in the air around us, which living things need to live

photosynthesis process by which plants make their own food using carbon dioxide, water and energy from sunlight

plankton microscopic organisms that live in the surface waters of the oceans

pollen male sex cell of a plant

pollination when pollen from one flower travels to the female parts of the same or different flower

prey animal that is caught and eaten by another animal

protein type of chemical that living things need for growth, maintenance and repair of their bodies

protists single-celled organisms that can only be seen under a microscope and mostly live in water

reproduction ability to produce offspring or young

respiration process by which living things release energy from their food

sexual reproduction when living things reproduce by fusing a male and a female sex cell

stimulus (plural **stimuli**) something that triggers or stimulates a reaction or response

stomata tiny openings on a leaf, usually on the underside

tissue group of cells connected together. They are linked with other tissues to form parts of the body.

Index

amoeba 5, 13, 22
animals 8, 10–13, 16, 18, 19, 21, 22, 25, 26, 29
asexual reproduction 6, 10

bacteria 6, 13, 15
bats 26
beetles 19, 29
breathing 16

carbon dioxide 11, 16, 19
carnivores, herbivores and omnivores 12
cells 5, 6, 7, 9, 10, 13, 15, 18, 26, 28, 29
coral 5

energy 4, 9, 11, 12, 15, 17, 19
excretion 4, 18-19
experiments 3, 14, 23, 27

faeces 19
fertilization 7, 8
fish 8, 16, 18, 26
flight 22
food chains 12
frogs 8, 10
fungi 13, 22

genes 10, 28
growth 4, 9-10

hydra 6

insects 7, 19, 26, 29

kelp 11

Leeuwenhoek, Anton van 28
life processes 4-5

lungs and gills 16, 19
mammals 8, 13, 18, 19
Mendel, Gregor 28
movement 4, 5, 20-3
muscles 5, 9, 15, 22

nutrients 11, 18, 19, 21
nutrition 4, 11-14, 18

oxygen 15, 16, 17, 19

photosynthesis 11–14, 17, 19, 24
plants 6, 7, 8, 10, 11, 12, 14, 17, 19, 20-1, 23, 24-5, 27, 29
pollen and pollination 7, 8, 20
predators and prey 12, 21, 26
protists 13, 22

reproduction 4, 6-8, 10, 20, 21
respiration 4, 15-17, 18, 19

seeds 7, 8, 20, 24
sense organs 25
sensitivity 4, 24-7, 29
sexual reproduction 7, 10
snakes 21, 26

tissues 9
trees 18, 29

urine 18

Venus flytrap 21

waste products 4, 18-19
water 13, 14
whales 16, 29

More books to read

Explore Science: Life Processes and Living Things, Angela Royston (Heinemann Library, 2003)
Life of Plants: Plant Growth, Louise and Richard Spilsbury (Heinemann Library, 2002)
Life Processes: Cells and Systems, Holly Wallace (Heinemann Library, 2001)
Life Processes: Survival and Change, Steve Parker (Heinemann Library, 2002)